Sally Cowan

Discover Japan!

Text: Sally Cowan
Publishers: Tania Mazzeo and Eliza Webb
Series consultant: Amanda Sutera
Hands on Heads Consulting
Editor: Kirstie Innes-Will
Project editor: Jarrah Moore
Designer: Leigh Ashforth
Project designer: Danielle Maccarone
Maps: Amanda Shufflebotham
Permissions researcher: Lumina Datamatics
Production controller: Renee Tome

Acknowledgements
We would like to thank the following for permission to reproduce copyright material:

Front cover: Stockbym/Adobe Stock Photos; p. 4 (bottom left): IamDoctorEgg/Shutterstock.com; p. 5 (bottom): eamesBot/Shutterstock.com; p. 6 (top right): Duy Phuong Nguyen/Alamy Stock Photo, (bottom right): robertharding/Alamy Stock Photo; p. 7 (top right): cowardlion/Shutterstock.com, (middle, bottom): CPA Media Pte Ltd/Alamy Stock Photo; p. 8 (top right): iStock.com/azuki25, (bottom right): iStock.com/davidf/Getty Images; p. 9 (top right): nadolu/Anadolu/Getty Images, (bottom): Ampika Muangthong/Shutterstock.com; p. 10 (bottom left): iStock.com/recep-bg/Getty Images; p. 11 (top right): Kirk Treakle/Alamy Stock Photo, (bottom): ULTRA.F/DigitalVision/Getty Images; p. 12 (top): Jim/Adobe Stock Photos, (bottom left): vkilikov/Shutterstock.com; p. 13 (bottom): Guitar photographer/Shutterstock.com; p. 15 (top right): VittoriaChe/Shutterstock.com, (bottom left): iStock.com/E+/tanukiphoto; p. 16 (top right): Newscom/Alamy Stock Photo, (bottom right): David Ball/Alamy Stock Photo; p. 17 (bottom): Archive Image/Alamy Stock Photo; p. 19 (left): Zoonar GmbH / Alamy Stock Photo, (right): Ilene MacDonald/Alamy Stock Photo; p. 20: ton koene/Alamy Stock Photo; p. 21 (top right): Everett Collection Inc/Alamy Stock Photo, (bottom): FiledIMAGE/Shutterstock.com; p. 22 (top right): iStock.com/Mila Naumova, (middle right, p. 1): akiyoko/Shutterstock.com, (bottom right): A. Zeitler/Adobe Stock Photos; p. 23 (top right): Carl Court/Getty Images Entertainment/Getty Images, (bottom right): a-clip/Getty Images; p. 24 (top): IamDoctorEgg/Shutterstock.com, (middle left/center): Birgit Reitz-Hofmann/Shutterstock.com, (middle right): Krivosheev Vitaly/Shutterstock.com, (bottom right): NooMUboN Photo/Shutterstock.com; p. 25: YOSHIKAZU TSUNO/Gamma-Rapho/Getty Images; p. 26 (top right): Torjrtrx/Shutterstock.com, (bottom right): Natsia27/Shutterstock.com; p. 27 (top right): kamui29/Shutterstock.com, (bottom): iStock.com/FG Trade; p. 28 (left): popular business/Shutterstock.com, (top right): Kosin Sukhum/Dreamstime.com, robtek/Shutterstock.com, Sakarin Sawasdinaka/Shutterstock.com, Tanya_mtv/Shutterstock.com, Mr. Nakorn/Shutterstock.com, (bottom right, p. 3): iStock.com/hanapon1002; p. 29 (top right): iStock.com/marketlan, (middle right): Gräfe & Unzer Verlag/Schütz, Anke/seasons.agency, (bottom right): Veronique Duplain/Shutterstock.com, (left): Enrique Díaz/7cero/Moment/Getty Images; p. 30 (top left): SeanPavonePhoto/Adobe Stock Photos, (middle left): J. Henning Buchholz/Shutterstock.com, (middle right): dzimmu/Shutterstock.com, (bottom right, back cover): silvester A F Diaz/Shutterstock.com, (bottom left): iStock.com/RichVintage.

NovaStar

ISBN 978 0 17 033483 9

Cengage Learning Australia
Level 5, 80 Dorcas Street
Southbank VIC 3006 Australia
Phone: 1300 790 853
Email: aust.nelsonprimary@cengage.com

For learning solutions, visit **cengage.com.au**

Printed in Malaysia by Papercraft
1 2 3 4 5 6 7 29 28 27 26 25

Nelson acknowledges the Traditional Owners and Custodians of the lands of all First Nations Peoples. We pay respect to Elders past and present, and extend that respect to all First Nations Peoples today.

Contents

Introducing Japan

Japan is a small country in North-East Asia. It is surrounded by sea but has some close neighbours, including China and South Korea.

Japan is an archipelago (pronounced *ar-kuh-pel-uh-go*), which is a group of islands that are close to each other. There are four main islands and thousands of small islands. Honshu is the largest island, where Japan's capital city, Tokyo, is located. The other main islands are Hokkaido, Kyushu and Shikoku.

Japan has many different environments, including snowy mountains, volcanoes, forests and low, flat plains. It has some unique wildlife, too.

Mount Fuji

Although Japan is about 20 times smaller than Australia, its population is almost 5 times bigger. People mostly live in large cities, but there are plenty of smaller towns. The cities and towns have modern and older buildings.

There is so much to discover about Japan, with its fascinating mix of old traditions and some of the most advanced technology found anywhere in the world.

Japan at a Glance!

Flag »

Land size » About 378 000 square kilometres

Main islands » Honshu, Hokkaido, Kyushu and Shikoku

Population » 125.7 million

Capital city » Tokyo

In Tokyo, on average over 2.4 million people cross the famous Shibuya Crossing every day.

People of Japan: Past and Present

People in the Past

Japan has a population of over 125 million people. In the past, most people were farmers, **homemakers**, traders and craftspeople.

For about 1500 years, an **emperor** has been the **head of state** in Japan. In the past, the emperor made laws for the whole country. There were some wealthy families, or **clans**, who managed their own lands.

The leaders of some clans became powerful **generals**, and the most powerful general in the land took the title of *shogun*. Some shoguns had more power than the emperors, and they ruled Japan for nearly 700 years, up until 1867.

The houses in this historic village of Shirakawa-go show visitors what life was like in Japan in the past.

Tokugawa Ieyasu was a powerful shogun in the early 1600s.

The emperor, the shogun and the clan leaders had armies of highly trained soldiers called *samurai* who helped carry out their laws. Most samurai were men, but some women became samurai too.

This statue is of a famous samurai, Kusunoki Masashige, who lived in the 14th century.

It took a long time for samurai to learn their skills in the **martial arts**, using swords, bows and arrows, and their hands and feet to fight. They had to toughen up their bodies and were taught to ignore hunger and cold, often walking barefoot in the snow. Their fighting skills and **honourable** behaviour made them highly respected in society.

Often, the samurai armies fought each other, but they also fought invaders. In the late 1200s, the samurai armies worked together to defeat the armies of Kublai Khan, a powerful emperor of China.

Tomoe Gozen was a famous female samurai general.

Royal Myth vs Fact

People used to say that all Japanese emperors were related to the **mythical** Emperor Jimmu from 600 **BCE**. Today, people agree that the royal family line can be traced back to 500 **CE** – which is still a very long line of related emperors!

People Today

More than 125 million people live in Japan today. Most people live in large cities, where skyscrapers containing apartments are close to schools and workplaces. There are also parks, shopping and entertainment areas, as well as **efficient** public transport. But many people live in smaller towns and villages too.

Sapporo is the largest city in Hokkaido.

Japanese people usually believe in doing what is best for society, rather than doing what is best for each individual person. So they have developed various **customs** that encourage people to treat each other with respect and patience. When people live so close together, these customs help society run smoothly without too much disagreement or disruption.

One respectful custom is bowing when greeting others, when thanking someone or when apologising for a mistake. Japanese people always try to be on time when meeting others, because they believe it is very rude to be late.

How Low Do You Go?

The lower someone bows, the more respect they show to the other person. From a young age, children learn to bow to their **elders**, including to their teachers.

Two women wearing traditional dress bow to one another.

The Government of Japan

Today, Japan is a **democratic** country. The people vote for their members of **parliament** from different political parties. These members then choose the prime minister to lead the government. People can vote after they turn 18.

Japan is what is known as a "constitutional monarchy". There is still an emperor, but he only performs **ceremonial** duties and has no power to make laws. The role of emperor is passed down to the eldest son (or other male relative if there are no sons).

the Emperor of Japan, Emperor Naruhito

The emperor and empress live in the Tokyo Imperial Palace.

Children in Japan

In Japan, children start school when they turn six. They learn a range of subjects, including reading and writing, mathematics, science, music and art. Students have to do homework most days.

There are three writing systems to learn in Japanese, each with their own set of **characters**, similar to letters in an alphabet. Students must learn all three systems. The most difficult one is called *kanji*. While the English alphabet has just 26 letters to learn, kanji has thousands of characters that can represent whole words or ideas.

School at a Glance!

Language spoken »
Japanese

School system »
primary school for 6 years;
middle school for 3 years;
high school for 3 years

Writing systems

- » *hiragana* (a set of 46 characters, based on sounds)
- » *katakana* (characters used to write words from other languages)
- » *kanji* (up to 8000 characters)

Many children go to homework clubs, where they continue to study for hours after school.

A Look at Kanji

By the time children finish their first six years of school, they know how to write about 1000 kanji characters. Some characters look like the ideas they represent, for example, this character means "tree":

Food education is also taught in Japan. Students learn about the importance of healthy eating habits in practical ways, for example, everyone eats the same school-made lunch in their classroom or canteen. The lunch is prepared by cooks who often use rice and vegetables that the students have grown in school gardens or helped farmers grow. Students take turns serving the hot foods to their friends, and everyone helps to clean up afterwards.

Children bring their own chopsticks and placemats to school for eating lunch.

Sport is an important part of school in Japan. Children play many different sports, both at school and in after-school clubs. Sports such as baseball and soccer are very popular.

Lots of Japanese children learn judo or karate, sports that developed from the old samurai martial arts.

The Land in Japan

Most of Japan is covered by mountains and forests. The mountains extend along the archipelago from north to south. In some places, the land slopes down from the mountains to low, flat plains beside the sea. There are cliffs, inlets and beaches along parts of the coast, with a variety of birds and sea creatures.

Golden eagles live in the lowlands of northern Japan, mostly on the islands of Hokkaido, Honshu and Kyushu.

Dugongs live in the sea around the most southern Japanese islands.

The Land at a Glance!

Mountains » cover about three-quarters of Japan.

Forests » cover about two-thirds of Japan.

Highest mountain » Mount Fuji, 3776 metres

Active volcanoes » 111

Volcanoes and Hot Springs

About three-quarters of the land in Japan is covered in mountains, many of which are volcanoes. Mount Fuji, on the island of Honshu, is the highest mountain. It is also an active volcano, but it hasn't erupted for more than 300 years. Scientists check Mount Fuji regularly for any signs of volcanic activity so that people can stay safe.

Mount Fuji is so high that it is often surrounded by clouds.

Awake or Asleep?

The terms "active" and "dormant" are used to describe volcanoes and are similar in meaning to "awake" and "asleep". An active volcano could erupt at any time. A dormant volcano hasn't erupted for a very long time, although an eruption could still happen.

Japan is located over an unstable part of Earth's **crust** where several **tectonic plates** meet. This is called a "fault line". Large amounts of molten hot rock, called "magma", lie close to Earth's surface between the tectonic plates. This is where volcanoes form, and there are about 111 active volcanoes in Japan, some out to sea but many of them on the main islands. They are constantly checked to see if they are likely to erupt soon.

In these volcanic areas, the hot magma also heats water that is under the ground. The water bubbles up to the surface in thousands of hot springs.

Many hot springs, called *onsens*, are used for the traditional custom of public bathing in Japan. To be an onsen, the water must be naturally heated to over 25° Celsius and contain certain substances that are good for the body. The soothing water also helps to relax muscles and calm the mind.

In the mountains near Nagano, Japanese macaque monkeys bathe in hot springs.

Onsens are usually separated into male and female areas.

Public Bathing at a Glance!

Some rules for bathing in an onsen include:

- Wash before getting in the onsen.
- Tie up long hair so that it doesn't get in the water.
- Don't splash!
- Avoid looking at other bathers you don't know.
- Speak quietly if bathing with family or friends.

Earthquakes

Apart from producing volcanoes and hot springs, Japan's fault line has other effects on the land. When the tectonic plates move and bump into each other, it causes earthquakes. Japan has about 1000 earthquakes a year. Most of them are small, but stronger ones can damage the land and buildings.

Homes, schools and skyscrapers in Japan are specially built to withstand most earthquakes. Japanese people have lots of information about how to stay safe during earthquakes, and children practise this from the time they start school.

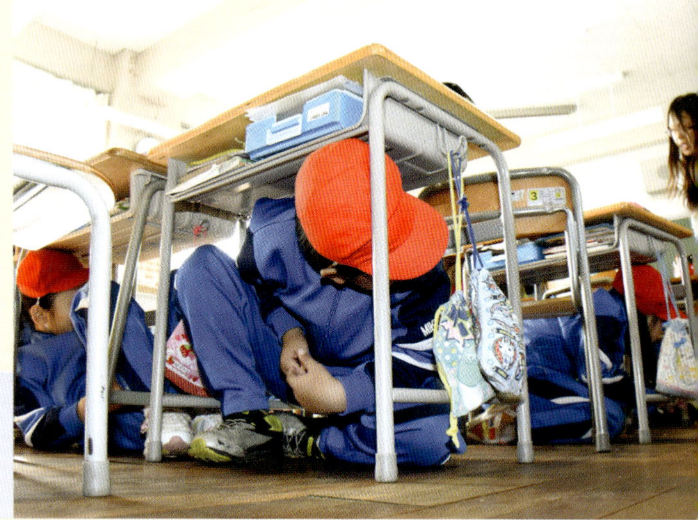

School children are taught to hide under their desks to stay safe if an earthquake occurs.

Shaking Rooms!

Sometimes schoolchildren visit special rooms that shake, as if an earthquake was happening. This training helps students become familiar with the feeling of an earthquake to stop them panicking when a real earthquake happens.

Children take turns experiencing the shaking room.

Tohoku – Japan's Strongest Earthquake at a *Glance!*

Date » 11 March 2011

Richter scale » 9.1 magnitude

Location » Pacific Ocean, 130 km off northern Honshu

Damage » The whole region shook and it was felt in Tokyo. The Tohoku earthquake:

- caused a tsunami that flooded land used for growing rice
- washed away cars and houses
- caused many deaths
- damaged the Fukushima Nuclear Power Plant, so people had to leave their homes for years; a large area is still not safe for people.

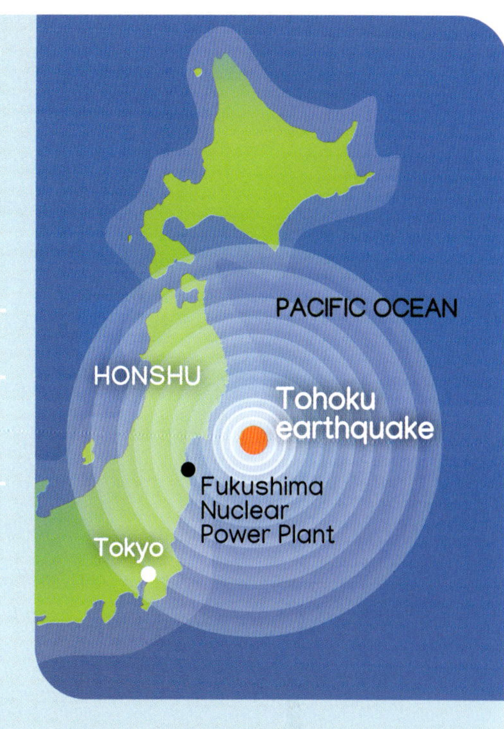

A tsunami caused widespread damage after the Tohoku earthquake.

Forests

Japan has many types of forests, from pine forests in snowy mountainous areas to rainforests in warmer parts of the country.

Other forests have **deciduous** maple trees. The ginkgo is another deciduous tree that has been in Japan for over 1000 years. In autumn, the leaves of the deciduous trees change colour and make brilliant displays of red, orange and yellow.

Tourists travel around Japan to see the cherry blossoms in forests, parks and gardens.

Japan's national flower blooms on one of the most spectacular trees of all: the sakura, or cherry blossom. In spring, sakura bloom in many shades of pink in forests, parks and gardens all over Japan.

Japan's deciduous maple and ginkgo trees are beautiful in autumn.

Gardens with Shrines and Temples

Japan is famous for its many beautiful and well-kept gardens, which often contain Shinto shrines and Buddhist temples. These places, with their traditional buildings, uncluttered garden designs, natural beauty and calm spaces give visitors feelings of wonder and wellbeing.

The rock garden at Ryoanji Buddhist Temple is famous for its calm, elegant design.

The entrances to Shinto shrines often have a *torii* gate, such as this famous one at Fushimi Inari Taisha in Kyoto.

Religion at a Glance!

There are two main religions in Japan, but people often have a mix of beliefs:

Shinto » a set of beliefs that developed in Japan, including **rituals** often practised at weddings

Buddhism » a religion that spread to Japan from China in the sixth century, with traditions often performed in funerals

Japanese Arts and Pastimes

Japan has many unique artforms and pastimes. Some are modern with a focus on entertainment, but others are traditional and have been practised for centuries.

Manga and Anime

Manga is a modern storytelling artform, with a focus on entertaining readers. Manga graphic novels have striking illustrations and not very much text.

The first manga was published in the early 1900s, but manga became very popular from the 1960s onwards. Today, reading manga is a popular pastime for adults and children. They can read all kinds of stories, including comedy, adventure, mystery and science fiction.

A manga artist, or *mangaka*, not only draws the illustrations but often writes the stories. In the past, mangaka drew on paper using only black ink to save time and printing costs. Today, a lot of drawing is done on digital screens. The mangaka might still draw in black, but now there are many manga studios where assistants add colour to the mangaka's drawings.

People enjoy browsing a wide range of manga in shops around Japan.

The art of anime is a type of animation that comes from the style of manga. The characters are drawn in bright colours, usually with large eyes that make it easy to see their emotions.

People of all ages enjoy watching different kinds of anime shows on television and anime movies at the cinema.

CRUNCHYROLL MOVIENIGHT PRESENTS

Sept 19, 22 & 23, 2018

HAIKYU!! THE MOVIE: BATTLE OF CONCEPTS

Haikyu!! is a popular sports anime series.

A popular pastime in Japan is called "cosplay", where young people dress up in costumes of their favourite manga and anime characters.

Manga at School

Manga is so popular in Japan that manga characters are even used in school textbooks to help students learn subjects such as science and history.

Ikebana

A traditional artform called *ikebana* is the art of arranging flowers according to many rules. Ikebana began centuries ago as a form of decoration for Buddhist temples. Today, many people enjoy doing ikebana as a pastime.

The flowers and leaves used in ikebana change with the seasons, but the arrangements must always show movement, **harmony** and balance.

The Japanese word "ikebana" means "living flowers".

Origami

Origami is the art of folding small squares of coloured paper to make shapes, such as animals or flowers. For hundreds of years, paper was a rare and precious item in Japan, and people thought it was wasteful to cut it. So, the art of origami was done using a whole sheet of paper. It was folded with much care and respect.

The most well-known origami shape is the crane, which is a large bird from Hokkaido.

Kabuki

A traditional style of theatre with stories from the past is called *kabuki*. Traditionally, the actors in kabuki are all men, who dress in striking make-up and costumes. The theatres have special features such as a revolving stage and a trapdoor. Traditional musical instruments are used to play the music for kabuki.

Kabuki actors often hold poses for several seconds and move in exaggerated ways.

Karaoke

A much newer pastime is karaoke, which began in the 1970s. People sing along to the music of popular songs in front of their friends. The singer has a microphone and can read the words of the song displayed on a screen.

Japanese people traditionally enjoy singing at social and business gatherings, so karaoke probably comes from this custom.

People go to private booths in specially designed karaoke buildings to sing karaoke.

Empty Orchestra!

The Japanese word "karaoke" translates to "empty orchestra" in English.

Vending Machines

The idea of using machines instead of people to do some easy jobs led to the development of a huge variety of vending machines in Japan. Instead of going to shops to buy products, people in Japan can buy them from vending machines on many streets, at any time of the day or night.

The machines dispense, or give out, hot and cold drinks and all kinds of snacks. Some machines dispense tasty meals, such as ramen noodles or hot chicken, as well as creamy desserts. Clothing vending machines dispense basic items such as t-shirts and underwear.

Vending Machines at a Glance!

How many? » About 5.5 million. That's one machine for every 23 people in Japan!

Since when? » Simple vending machines became popular in the 1950s.

Video Games

Japan has produced some of the most popular video games and **consoles** ever made. This started with the coin-operated game *Space Invaders* in 1978, and soon led to the development of personal video game consoles that people could have in their own homes.

Japanese video game designers were responsible for worldwide hits such as *Super Mario Bros* and *Pokémon*. These designers have shaped the huge gaming industry that exists today.

Food in Japan

In different parts of Japan, people eat a range of foods, usually including fish, meat or tofu, and fresh or pickled vegetables. Meals can include rice or noodles and are often served with miso soup.

Japan is surrounded by sea, so fish, seafood and seaweed are popular ingredients. Sushi is mounds of cold rice topped with raw fish, egg or vegetables – it's one of Japan's most famous foods and has become popular around the world.

The bento box is a Japanese invention, containing a meal for one person in a box.

In Japan, it is considered good manners to sip soup from a bowl and make slurping sounds.

How to Make Vegetable Sushi Rolls

Goal

To make delicious and healthy sushi rolls

Equipment

» a bamboo sushi mat or a clean tea towel folded in half

» a water bowl, for dipping fingers

» a vegetable knife

Ingredients

» 1 cup of cooked sushi rice, cooled

» nori (seaweed) sheets

» 1 small cucumber, cut in long thin slices

» ½ an avocado, sliced

» 1 small carrot, cut in long thin slices

Change Up Your Sushi

You can add your favourite fillings, such as tinned tuna, smoked salmon or fried tofu, to the vegetables in this sushi roll.

Steps

1. Place a sheet of nori on the sushi mat.
2. Use your hands to spread the rice onto the nori sheet in a layer about 1 centimetre thick. Dip your hands into the water bowl as you press, because the rice can be very sticky!
3. Leave 3 centimetres at one edge of the nori sheet to allow the roll to be sealed.
4. Place the vegetables on the rice in a row.
5. Pick up the edge of the sushi mat and roll it over once. Then press the nori tightly.

6. Gently roll the nori, then press the edge to seal the sushi roll.
7. Ask an adult to cut the sushi roll into even pieces.
8. Serve with a small bowl of soy sauce for dipping.

Much More to Discover!

Japan is a country with many unique and interesting features, from its land to its food. Its people have a wide variety of customs, arts and pastimes. This has just been a small taste of Japan – there is so much more to discover!

More ... at a Glance!

Himeji Castle

Castles » sometimes shoguns and samurai had their own castles

Sumo wrestling » Japan's national sport, with many ancient rituals

Pottery » one of the oldest arts, used to make all sorts of pots, plates and jugs from clay

Kimono » the national dress of Japan, a loose robe with square sleeves, tied with a wide belt

Bonsai » the traditional art of growing normally large plants, such as trees, in small pots using special pruning and shaping methods

Glossary

artificial intelligence (AI) (*noun*) the ability of computers to do tasks that are usually done by people, like writing text or making art

BCE (*adjective*) Before the Common Era; the number of years before the time dates are counted from

CE (*adjective*) years since the beginning of the Common Era

ceremonial (*adjective*) relating to religious or cultural events

characters (*noun*) written symbols that represent words or sounds

clans (*noun*) extended family groups

consoles (*noun*) electronic devices for playing video games

crust (*noun*) the outer layer of Earth, made of rock

customs (*noun*) common practices of a particular group of people

deciduous (*adjective*) a tree or plant that loses its leaves each year in autumn

democratic (*adjective*) related to a system of government where everyone votes

efficient (*adjective*) fast, effective and not wasteful

elders (*noun*) older people

emperor (*noun*) the male ruler of an empire

generals (*noun*) senior army officers

harmony (*noun*) when things are pleasingly consistent

head of state (*noun*) the top representative of a country; as in Japan, the head of state might not be the leader of the government

homemakers (*noun*) people who look after the home

honourable (*adjective*) honest, fair and worthy of respect

martial arts (*noun*) particular sets of fighting and self-defence skills

mythical (*adjective*) from old traditional stories rather than history

parliament (*noun*) a group of people with the power to make laws

rituals (*noun*) ceremonies or actions performed in a set way

tectonic plates (*noun*) the huge slabs of rock that make up Earth's crust

Index